Black Nerd, Blue Box
THE WIBBLY WOBBLY MEMOIRS OF A LONELY WHOVIAN

T. Aaron Cisco

Copyright © 2019, Taylor A. Cisco, III

All rights reserved.

ISBN: 9781088471418

Dedicated to all nerds everywhere, across time and space

WE'RE ALL STORIES

"I'm nobody."

"There's nothing wrong with that statement. It's merely a fact. It's the kind of phrase that has negative connotations, but it shouldn't really."

"Exactly. When you stop and think about it, the overwhelming majority of people you meet are nobody, and I'm no different."

"Only a fraction of the human population are really *somebody* in the colloquial sense. Or to put a slightly more positive spin on the sentiment, everyone you've evet met, ever will meet, and quite frankly, are meeting right now, is literally somebody, so by laws of logic, then everyone is nobody. Kind of like, if everyone is beautiful then no one is."

"That's a good point. Granted, everybody is somebody to somebody, but at the same time, everybody is also nobody to somebody. The hard part isn't figuring out whether someone you meet is somebody or nobody to you, nor is it a matter of figuring out whether you're somebody or nobody to them. The important question to answer is whether you are somebody or nobody to yourself."

"But if you're nobody, who the hell am I?"

"Nobody to most, somebody to few."

"So, we're the same?"

"Of course."

"But we're conversing."

"No, this is a one-sided dialogue."

"One-sided dialogue? So, this conversation is entirely internal? What the hell kind of memoir is this?"

"It's my memoir."

"Right on."

"But back to the original question."

"Who am I?"

"To most people, I think it's safe to say that I'm nobody. I know that this entire thing began with that statement, so to avoid further repetition, I'll elaborate."

"Please do."

"If someone passed by me, while waiting in the queue for a slightly overpriced soy latte at my neighborhood's franchise of a national coffeehouse chain, it's unlikely that you'd recall doing so. I'm tall, but only one to three inches taller than the average American man, depending on who's counting. My census demographic is African-American- or Black, to be more precise- but that same box is checked by over forty-two million other Americans."

"So, I'm somebody, just not a notable somebody?"

"No, that would be an exercise in wanton arrogance, a measure of self-aggrandizing delusion feeding an ego so inflated, that all the postings and pictures of the collective social sites on the internet aren't enough to satiate my narcissistic tendencies."

"I get it. Like, who the hell am I that I should sit down and write a collection of memoirs?"

"Precisely."

"I'm nobody."

"And that's the point?"

"I'm not saying that I am unimportant, or that most people are unimportant. Remember that episode in which the Eleventh Doctor said that in nine hundred years of time and space, he'd never met anyone who wasn't important?"

"Of course!"

"Well, I haven't been around anywhere near that long, but I agree. Everyone is important. Importance and status aren't mutually exclusive, nor are they necessarily accompanying either."

"That's a bit snarky."

"Would I be anything else?"

"Touché."

"Moving on. Every nanosecond of every day, we experience situations that change us. Some of these situations are imperceivably small. Some unavoidably huge, but the only way be you is to know you, and to know you is to know what combination of occurrences melded together to yield what you are now."

"So, you are what you've been through."

"Now you're getting it. The human body is an amazing entity, given the ability to heal one's self based on inner wisdom. While I don't believe that all internal maladies can be remedied with a healthy dollop of introspection, I can confidently say that there is in fact, something quite remarkable that occurs when you decide to unlock the cages of hindsight in order to let loose the experiences and stories that led you to your current point."

"Wow, do I really talk like this?"

"That probably came off a bit more metaphysical and "new-agey" than I intended, but the overall gist is the reason why someone like me, a nobody, has taken pen to paper (or fingertips to keyboard, to be exact) to unleash nearly four decades of recollections, curated around a near-lifelong fandom is a twofold endeavor."

"I fully understand. On one hand, it is in fact cathartic, in some ways. By forcing myself to recall and write down the experiences that I...uh, experienced, I'm able to view them through a different lens. A lens that is definitely older- although not necessarily wiser in every case- but by changing the perspective via distance, it has allowed me to realign and redefine the impact those moments, both positive and negative."

"Yes…"

"And on the other hand, by making my stories of being nobody available to others who may also be questioning whether they are nobody to themselves, then perhaps that they'll find something within these pages that'll help them to realign and redefine the impact of their own experiences. The most positive aspect of being a nobody to most others besides yourself, is one of the most overlooked."

"And that is?

"That I have company."

"Yes, I do."

"Whether it's one, one hundred, or one thousand people comprising that company doesn't matter. It's the fact that I'm not an anomaly. I'm not alone in the universal sense, and that counts for a lot more than a lot of people realize."

"And solitude amid the masses-can be devastating, especially when that crowd seems to share common traits and interests."

"We may have never met, and there's a possibility that we might never meet. But perhaps you can relate to the awkward experiences of a somewhat witty, definitely verbose, unquestionably awkward, nerdy Black kid wholly captivated by a TV show staring a time travelling alien in a blue box. In which case, we can be nobody together."

"That last bit was for the reader, yeah?"

"Yeah, it was."

"Groovy?"

"Groovy."

BLACK NERD, BLUE BOX

I MIGHT HAVE MISCALCULATED

It was supposed to be just another boring Saturday morning. Wake up. Cartoons. Brush teeth. Eat breakfast. We'd spent the remainder of the morning, dropping off dry cleaning, picking up groceries, and paying bills. Luckily, I had grabbed some comic books, markers, and a sketch pad to brace myself for the unbearable boredom of being a largely involuntary companion to my parents' mundane but necessary adventures across the city and suburbs.

When we got home, we settled into our typical weekend routine. This was existence as I knew it at the time. I was mostly unaware and completely uninterested in the habits of other families. It wasn't that I was oblivious. I was, quite honestly, completely content with our familial standard.

My Ma and Dad did grownup stuff, while my kid sister and I played with our toys on the floor in the front room. This Saturday afternoon though? This Saturday wasn't like the others. This was the Saturday afternoon, that I saw Doctor Who for the first time. The episode was Paradise Towers.

I don't know what made me pay attention, but there was something about that episode that resonated with me. I was already somewhat aware of Doctor Who, but I wasn't even a casual fan yet. Though it was probably inevitable. Both of my parents had been Whovians since the Tom Baker era. My Ma even knit my Dad a faithful version of his iconic scarf back when they were dating. It was predestined. It would only be a matter of time before I'd discover what tens of millions around the world already knew: Doctor Who is amazing!

That Paradise Towers was my gateway episode made a lot of sense. Paradise Towers had a massive variety of elements that appealed to my second-grade sensibilities.

The plot centers around the Seventh Doctor (played by the inimitable, Sylvester McCoy) and his Companion, Mel Bush (played by the incomparable Bonnie Langford) discovering a swimming pool in a majestic, alien, high rise complex sometime in the far future. They quickly find that the luxurious residence is an architectural wasteland, with dangers around every turn- including a terrifying, noncorporeal monster hiding in the basement.

There are warring gangs using the halls as their battlefields. Devious cannibals luring unsuspecting prey to a grisly demise in their unassuming apartments. Hell, there was even a robot-lobster-octopus thing lurking in the swimming pool. And of course, there was the horrific monster waiting down in the basement eating whatever unfortunate residents were fed to it by the buzz saw-wielding, robotic centurions known ominously as Cleaners.

What seven-year-old geek wouldn't be transfixed by a time traveling alien and his striking companion, taking on these threats, as well as an evil army of Nazis-esque villains working for a shadowy creature lurking in the shadowy lower levels?

For a kid who'd who loved science, Star Trek, ZooBooks magazine, Goosebumps, and Scary Stories to Tell in the Dark, this episode checked all my entertainment boxes. It was almost as though the writers and producers at the BBC had attached a hose to the part of my preadolescent brain containing the overflowing, eclectic tank where my entertainment tastes were stored, cranked the lever, and blasted the contents across the screen.

Way before TiVo and digital recorders made capturing shows the standard for the average TV viewer, my Dad used to record numerous programs on the VCR. Thanks to his delightful willingness to convert hours of programming into miles of tape, I was able to indulge and cultivate my burgeoning Whovian fandom through repeated viewings.

I was so excited by my new-found obsession that on Monday, I made an irreparable social faux pas. I eagerly attempted to spread the good news of Doctor Who during Spelling Class.

Even at the young age of seven, I was already on the outside of whatever it was that the in-crowd was inside of, so I should've known better, but I thought that with something as amazing as Doctor Who, I'd be able to create an opening in that impenetrable wall of elementary school popularity.

Nobody had ever explicitly told me why I wasn't accepted among my pears and I was too inobservant to decipher (the numerous) clues on my own. I was tall for my age, but not interested in athletes or sports. It wasn't like I was opposed to competitive recreation. I loved chess, but that didn't count apparently.

Even though I enjoyed building models, taking things apart, and staring at the schematics in the pages of Popular Science magazine, I couldn't care less about collecting posters of sports cars, or going to the air show to watch daredevil pilots in noisy jets.

I hadn't yet found refuge in the creative arts at that point either. I was a fan of music, but apparently it was the wrong kind of music. Having had three years of piano under my prepubescent belt at the time, I was already unimpressed with the over-produced, paint-by-numbers pop music blasting from seemingly every radio. I dug the virtuosos and jazz cats- the same stuff my parents had been digging on for years.

I'd beg them to play their records, whining, wearing them down, though honestly, I think they enjoyed having a kid who dug the same tunes they did. When they didn't have time to set up and play their records, I made mixtapes- dozens of mixtapes- taping and re-taping over cassettes, sitting patiently next to the old stereo, listening to the oldies station, rolling my eyes when the DJ talked over the intro or faded out before the song was all the way finished.

I mean, I was aware of the more popular music of course. It was the Eighties, the birthplace of multimedia oversaturation. And truth be told, I even liked some of it. But who's got time to bop around to Jody Watley and Debbie Gibson when Jimi Hendrix is wailing on Machine Gun, and Pretty Purdie is grooving on Funky Donkey?

Tiffany? Bananarama? No thanks. Not when I've got Leonard Bernstein conducting the New York Philharmonic with the most perfect rendition of Gershwin's Rhapsody in Blue, and Wendy Carlos adding contemporary flair to the Baroque styles, playing Air on a G String, Chorale Prelude, and ten other classic pieces by Bach on a Moog synthesizer.

Mine was an equal-opportunity repudiation. It didn't matter if they were White kids, Asian kids, other Black kids, LatinX, or Indian, they didn't dig me. It didn't matter if they lived in the suburbs or the city. It didn't matter whether their families were rich, poor, or middle class. No matter who they were, or where they were from, the kids didn't want anything to do with this cappuccino-colored oddball.

I was deeply into Star Trek and had just discovered the incomparable awesomeness of Wonder Woman comics a few months prior. So, I already had two strikes against me. It was a risky, social gamble to try and present this odd, British program about an alien in a time machine as something so cool they couldn't help but welcome me into the fold as one of their own, but I didn't have much to lose.

At this point, the physical bullying hadn't really taken off yet. I was pushed around a little bit, but my primary school torment was still in the preliminary stages of random name-calling and general avoidance, due to what I erroneously believed to be nothing more than a simple matter of disparate interests. Paradise Towers was going to fix that.

Doctor Who was going to be my entry into that all too exclusive club of second grade social acceptance. Robots, monsters, aliens, action, suspense and violence…if they thought Captain Eo (*the Disney World 3D movie starring Michael Jackson, written by George Lucas, and directed by Francis Ford Coppola*) was really the most- as so many of them did- then this Doctor Who show was going to blow their minds.

I wasn't completely reckless. I knew better than to just announce it to my classmates at random. I had to wade in. There was a girl who sat in front of me that wasn't completely awful. She'd never called me any bad names, and on the field trip, she didn't make a face when the only empty seat on the school bus was next to me. She wasn't nice to me really, but she wasn't super mean. I figured that was good enough.

"Hey." I whispered, tapping her desk.

"Oh, um, what do want Taylor? And why do you have question marks on your shirt?" she asked reasonably, squinting with annoyed curiosity.

"Have you heard of Doctor Who?"

"Doctor what?"

"Not Doctor *what*, Doctor *Who*!"

"Is this a…game?"

"No, it's a game. It's a show."

"A show called Doctor Who?"

"Yeah! It's about this alien guy named Doctor! That's what the question marks on my shirt are for. It's my own Doctor Who question mark vest!"

"Question mark vest? That's not a vest. That's like five question marks you drew on your shirt in pencil."

Okay, in her defense, she's kind of right. I probably shouldn't have crudely drawn a bunch of question marks on my shirt. But in my defense, this was the Eighties. Sure, nowadays you can just stroll into any Target, Macy's, Hot Topic, or other retail chain and pick up any number of officially licensed caps, bags, shirts, buttons, and bedsheets. And if they don't have your fandom, a few seconds online will get you whatever you want, from any franchise you want.

But back then, the amount and access to licensed, branded content was nowhere near as abundant, so DIY was the only way to go. And understandably, my skills as a preadolescent cosplayer were somewhat lacking in execution.

"I know, but listen, he's got a time machine, and he fights monsters and robots and---"

"Why are you so weird?"

"I'm not weird."

"You drew on your shirt."

"I thought it was--"

"Teacher! Taylor is bothering me! He drew on his shirt, and I think he's going to draw on me next!"

"I'm not bothering you! I'm not drawing on you!"

Our teacher came over and bent down to my level. That was what she did whenever she had to address someone in the class. I think she thought it made us feel more comfortable since we wouldn't have to crane our necks to look up at her, but it was intimidating.

"Mr. Cisco. What is so important you felt the need to disrupt the entire classroom by bothering her?"

"I wasn't bothering her. Just talking about a show."

"A show?"

"Doctor Who."

"Doctor Who?"

"Yeah, it's really cool! Have you seen it?"

"That's enough Mr. Cisco!"

"But…"

"Mr. Cisco! Please gather your things and go to the office. While you're there, think about whether class time is the appropriate time to try and impress your little crush."

"Crush? What? No, I was just talking about the cool Doctor Who show, and…"

"Now, Mr. Cisco."

"But…"

"Now!"

I shoved my class materials into my Trapper Keeper, trying to ignore the snickers from my classmates. The two other black children in my class had a slight glint of empathy behind their stares. We weren't really friends, but the three of us possessed that inherent sense of general solidarity that comes from being distinctive in an environment that demands conformity. It's the same unspoken commonality that yields casual cultural customs like "the nod."

But they didn't dare show support for this gangly oddball. And I couldn't blame them. The stakes were too high. We were still years away from developing the confidence required to defy the status quo- even if the specific status quo we'd be defying was one that still had bedtimes, were Santa believers, and a shoe-tying proficiency that was only slightly above novice.

I did notice however, that even though they didn't help or defend me, they also didn't laugh. For me, that display of passive empathy was something.

It's been decades, but the cruel cacophony of my classmates' ridicule hasn't died down. Sure, it's a hell of a lot easier to ignore, but I can still hear it just as clearly now, as it was then.

I trudged down the hallway, listening to my footsteps punctuate the low murmur of other classes. Before reaching the office, I stopped in the bathroom and washed the question marks off my shirt.

In most memoirs, this is the point where I'm supposed to describe how that moment triggered some mild epiphany that altered the course of my prepubescence, contributing a foundational stone upon which my current outlook is built. But I didn't *learn* anything from that moment. It didn't alter the course of my prepubescence. It was merely further confirmation of what I'd already known.

The next day, and for the remainder of elementary and middle school, nothing changed. I was still "weird." I was still the primary target of contempt and derision. Hell, I still drew on my shirts sometimes.

What did change that day, however, was that when I got home, I was able to ease my alienation with a trip across time and space, to a rendezvous at Paradise Towers, where I could see The Doctor. Free from ridicule, I could admire his bravery, his humor, and that sweet question mark vest.

T. AARON CISCO

THE ILLUSION IS ALWAYS ONE OF NORMALITY

"Wow, that was a really sad way to begin this book."

"What the hell? I'm back again?"

"Of course, I'm back. Where would I go?"

"I don't know. I just figured that since the memories part of the memoir had begun, that I'd just let the recollections speak for themselves."

"Where I go is where I am. I can't go anywhere that I'm not. This is a one-sided dialogue, remember?"

"Right."

"That question-mark vest incident."

"What about it?"

"Sad, wasn't it?"

"Very."

"And that's it?"

"That was all there was. I dove wholeheartedly into Doctor Who fandom. Head first, no floatation device, no raft, no lifeguard. And when I tried to inform others about how incredibly groovy it was, I was misunderstood, mocked, and alienated."

"And bullied."

"Well, obviously."

"Was it that obvious?"

"I mean, it's a memoir. The most important aspect of that particular incident was the origination of what would become a lifelong passion. It wasn't the years of torment that followed."

"But the torments were important as well."

"Yeah, but nerdy kid getting picked on for being nerdy isn't a story. It's a cliché."

"That depends on how it's framed."

"What other way is there to frame it?"

"I was asking for it. Now I know that victim blaming is horrendous, and rightfully frowned upon but allow me to clarify."

"Please do!"

"I'm not saying I deserved to be attacked, or that the bullies were justified. I'm saying, I knew what the consequences were for being outside the norm and chose not to hide who I was. Not that I had much choice. Honesty can sometimes lead to tragedies."

"That's a fair point. I suppose, considering how much of an unrepentant geek I was, it would've been surprising if I *hadn't* been bullied."

"It is a well-known fact that bullies often target people they can easily intimidate and threaten. And children who are unable for one reason of another to mix well and get along as a group will eventually be left to their own devices, thus making them an ideal target for bullies."

"Would I have rather not been the subject of mockery and minor, physical assaults? Of course. I meet people all the time who say that they were practically invisible in high school, and stare at them with the kind of wide-eyed envy usually reserved for cartoonish portrayals of gold-diggers in bad movies."

"But I didn't really want to be invisible."

"Well, considering height, weight, tastes, and personal style (or lack thereof), invisibility isn't exactly a status that could've ever been achieved."

"It wasn't that I wanted to be invisible in the sense that nobody noticed. I wanted to at least be able to give the illusion that I was normal. Sort of, disappear into the crowd, rather than being alone in it."

"I was normal."

"Was I?"

"Well, I wasn't odd."

"Nonconformist, then?"

"Well not really that either. I didn't deliberately set out to be strange or different. I did what everyone else did. I liked what I liked. But by pursuing my genuine interests, since those interests weren't what the other kids in my immediate area were interested in, it made for a natural distinction."

"Being true to self, may leave you by yourself."

"That's a horribly unclever adage."

"It's kind of clever."

"No, it's like the trash you see on social sites where someone takes a picture of themselves sitting on a beach, looking out over the water with a constipated look on their face, and caption it with something like: *our paths are different, but I'm not lost.*"

"I'm still going to type it aren't I?"

"Ugh, yeah. All I wanted to do was share an amazing TV show. When something is a source of happiness- I mean genuine happiness- I want to share it. Like say for instance that I find an amazing restaurant, great food, great atmosphere, the prices are reasonable? I don't keep it a secret, I tell everyone. I like to think that most people feel the same way too."

"I think they do. But I also think that when you're talking about children in primary school, the repercussions for sharing any source of happiness that deviates from the norm can be soul-crushing."

"It really is a sad way to start the book."

"Something a little lighter then? Sort of a literary palate cleanser to wash the image of a sad young nerd made to be the laughing stock of the entire class out of the reader's minds?"

"I've got just the thing."

"Groovy."

THICKTOWN, THICKANIA

The line between self-acceptance and self-delusion is only a few nanometers wide, so you can almost excuse the average person for conflating the two. But regardless of widespread misconceptions to the contrary, they are in fact, opposing philosophies.

Self-delusion is much more comfortable, hence the rampant popularity, but self-acceptance is a far healthier state of mind- even if it is infinitely harder. Especially when the traits, habits, and quirks that you must accept about yourself lead to one conclusion: that you're a Nerd.

Being a Nerd is hard. Of course, it is. The concept of humans as a communal species is so unanimously accepted, it's practically indisputable. To be an outsider amongst billions of insiders is more than just socially stigmatic, it's dangerous at an evolutionary level.

The collective is considered an absolute necessity, so it stands to reason that to be separate from the collective, whether voluntarily or not, is to invite an innumerable horde of professional hazards and interpersonal tribulations. Being a Nerd isn't just hard. Being a Nerd can be dangerous.

But the silver lining piercing the dark clouds of social rejection is the fact that nerds can hide their nerdiness. In order to shed the damning label of "geek", all you have to do is fake it. Repress your actual interests and reserve the true nature of your personality for when nobody else is around.

Western culture bows at the temple of the ostensible. When faced with proof of the inauthentic, people love to call it out. At the same time, we produce mountains of media calling for others to "just be themselves," but the plain truth is that we adore frauds. So, while being a nerd is hard, it is easily hidden.

Being Black is hard. Yes, I'm fully aware of how ridiculous that sentence is. It may be the single biggest understatement in the history of written and spoken language. Imagine if there were such a thing as a hardness chart. Picture a scale or infographic designed solely to quantify the obstacles and hazards experienced by every American group on an hourly basis. Being Black wouldn't be on the chart. It would be too high measure. Like trying to weigh an elephant with a postage scale, the units of measurement wouldn't be anywhere near sufficient.

That's not to say that any individual identity or group demographic is free from challenges, or has it easy, but rather that the amount of adversity is comparatively disproportionate to those of any individual identity or group demographic that contains Black as a descriptor.

It should go without saying, but unlike Nerdiness, Blackness cannot be hidden. There's historical precedent for many who have tried- most commonly via "passing"- but for every instance of passing of which we're aware, exactly one-hundred percent of them failed. If those passing folks had been successful, we wouldn't have known that those folks had been passing. This, among trillions of other reasons, is why being Black is astoundingly harder than being a Nerd.

So, what happens when you're both Black and a Nerd? What happens when no matter what you do or say, or pretend to be depending on the people around you, and/or what the situation requires, you'll always be an "other?"

Well, that's when the difference between self-acceptance and self-delusion becomes more than just important, it becomes a prerequisite for daily life.

One of the most challenging aspects of adopting a sense of self-acceptance is dealing with those who haven't. To them, your internal awareness and honesty pulls back the curtain on their hypocrisy. It threatens to expose and erode the façade they work so tirelessly to maintain, which triggers a negative reflex in them.

In some cases, it's merely embarrassment. Midway through my professional career, I was in a meeting and the person running it had built a reputation on their acute insights into issues of equity and race. I was new on the committee- and the only colored crayon in the box, so to speak- so the head of the meeting wanted to show off their skills in "understanding the experiences of people of color," and what better way to demonstrate just how far they could walk in my low SPF shoes, then by "cold reading" my autobiography.

If you're unaware, cold reading is a sort of short cut to knowing someone. It's kind of an advanced parlor trick used by skilled politicians, corporate consultants, and scam artists (yes, I realize of course those three can, and often are, one in the same) to give the illusion that you know more information about a person, than they have explicitly given.

The average person uses more than a few cold reading indicators every day. If for instance, you meet someone who has a southern accent when they speak, you'd assume that they were from the south. The tricky part, and where a lot of sloppy and/or cocky people get caught up is in drawing the line between educated guessing and broad generalities.

Assuming a childhood spent below the Mason Dixon line based on speech inflection is one thing. Assuming that because of that childhood, the person came from a certain economic background, or holds specific political or religious beliefs is another.

The head of the committee was in the latter camp...

"Before we get started, I'd like to introduce the new member of the committee." She smiled warmly, waving her hand, gesturing for me to stand.

"Hello everyone," I stood and nodded, "Glad to be part of the group. I look forward to--"

"Taylor here is an asset," she continued, interrupting, "not just professionally, but also, as you can see, he's a proud person of color."

Had she stopped there it would've just been mildly awkward. It's a weird thing to say, but not inaccurate.

I *am* proud of my professional achievements. I *am* a Person of Color. I don't try to hide or downplay those facts. But it's weird hearing someone introduce you with such broad generalities. It'd be like if I was introducing you to my kids and said, 'these are my daughters, I made them via copulation.' You'd be like, 'yeah, I guess, but what the hell?' Just because it's true, doesn't mean it needs to be shared.

"Thank you." I muttered retaking my seat.

"Wait a moment," the meeting head persisted, "Keep standing. I want everyone to see you."

"Um, okay." I replied, standing back up.

"Taylor here is an incredible success story. Raised in a dangerous neighborhood, probably to a single mother. He had to overcome so much pressure- poverty, drugs, threats of gang violence. But look at him now! He's living proof that with the right mindset, and access to opportunities, the communities we serve aren't filled with thugs and criminals, they're just like everyone else in this room. Taylor, could you please take a few moments and share your story?"

"Really?"

"Yes, please."

As cynical, and world-weary as I am, I was shocked. Not at her passive racism- I've met many bigots of every age, color, and economic standing- but rather at her bold arrogance. She wasn't just incredibly inaccurate in her assumption, but she so incredibly confident in what was basically impromptu fan-fiction.

The face of my colleague, a work friend who was also at the meeting, went pale. She knew me, so she knew that everything that had just come out of the meeting head's mouth was complete and utter garbage. She also knew, that while I had a thick skin, I was not above unleashing a firehose of snarky truth when the need arose. Her expression wasn't of fear or sympathy, but rather cautious anticipation.

"Sure, I can share my story." I smiled devilishly.

"Thank you! The floor is yours."

"Well," I began with a completely straight face, "my mother had to raise my sister and I alone…for a couple hours after school until my dad got home from work. And there was so much pressure. Would I go to downstate for undergrad and then come back for my Master's and Doctorate like they did? Or go abroad like my grandparents did when they finished college?"

The meeting head was embarrassed, but it was their own fault. Broad generalizations are what dumb people use to make themselves seem more intelligent, not realizing the results are the exact opposite. And when broad generalizations are applied to a ridiculous notion like identity, then it's a whole other level of vacuity.

And it's not just some out-of-touch, overconfident, executive types making these assumptions. Even in the seemingly progressive and open-minded world of entertainment, there were still instances in which the casual ignorance of broad generalities tainted the vibe.

What I learned was that even though physically, geographically, we were hundreds of miles north of the Mason-Dixon line, the attitudes and philosophies most commonly associated with the mid-Sixties South, were just as prevalent here at home.

BLACK NERD, BLUE BOX

TALKING ABOUT MY GENERATION

"I suggest something more light-hearted and the results were examples of casual, professional racism?"

"Yes. That's what those were."

"How is that light-hearted?"

"Well, the racists in the previous memory were embarrassed. So, although it's not exactly a comedic recollection, it's a bit of schadenfreude via hindsight."

"Is that funny?"

"It's not, not-funny."

"The racism-free racists are so pervasive though, at this point, it's almost mundane. I mean the staggering amount of people who cling to that self-hypocrisy festering in their minds when it comes to the notions of the wholly fictional, and overwhelmingly superfluous, American concept of race, it's practically the default setting for the country."

"Is there anything more contemporarily American than the deeply held doublethink?"

"Jesus, I thought this was something people were supposed to outgrow. Weren't posers- especially enlightened posers- something that died decades ago?"

"Posers never go out of style. And enlightened posers has been the new hotness since…well, ever."

"Remember when I wrote that Op-ed complaining about Wokie-Dopes a decade or so ago?"

"The term 'wokie-dope' wasn't really around back then, but yeah, I pretty much remember most of what I've written."

"How did it go again?"

"Really?"

"I think the readers will dig it."

"Okay, but just an excerpt. This is supposed to be my memoirs, not a collection of old writing…from January 6, 2008, originally written for…"

"What are you doing?"

"Citation."

"But I wasn't paid for the original piece."

"Well yeah, it was just an unsolicited Op-ed, but they still published it."

"Couldn't I just add an acknowledgement at the end of the book, or footnote at the end of this segment?"

"I will."

"It feels like I'm stalling. Just get on with it."

"Fine. But again, just an excerpt…"

"In order to be considered one of 'us' you've got to start behaving like one of 'them.' The revolution will not be televised, but the rights have already been optioned and I hear that the actress who used to date the musician who was married to the author but was secretly dating the actor who just came out of the closet and is now being linked to the former secretary of something or other is sort of, but not quite possibly linked to star or direct or produce or mention it in his and her and their next press junket."

Remember to abstain from watching A-list films because God forbid you be entertained by anything other than obscure, subtitled and not necessarily well-produced or even well-researched drivel that the director-slash-writer-slash-activist who wears vintage jeans, second-hand shoes and antique glasses (but somehow still manages to spend half a million dollars on his/her wardrobe) released in only forty-five cities to maintain credibility, but conveniently forgets to mention all the independent papers, that the distribution house that delivered the prints to those forty-five cities is same one that releases the A-list films you're not supposed to watch.

When visiting the grocery store, please keep in mind that though it's cheaper and by definition, it's pretty much the exact same thing, you must avoid purchasing any item that does not contain the words "organic" or "free-range" or some lengthy description of the principles the company strongly adheres to in order to save and maintain the environment, as they're loading their products on the gas-guzzling, air-poisoning flatbeds and semitrucks and airplanes. The fact that my chickens and cows had happy lives, my milk comes from a plant instead of an udder and my grains were farmed by farmers who can't afford to incorporate is well worth the extra ten to eighty dollars a month towards my grocery expenses.

We'll all join hands and rage against the machine, and bitch about the current administration. Ignore the fact that it's an administration we put into power in the first place. It's not our fault that we ignored (twice!) a basic aspect of political science. Bipartisan means three or four or nine parties, right? Who cares if I'm splitting the vote? The grooviest Myspace page deserves our votes. It's not a matter of winning or losing, it's all about how you play the game and as long as your game piece has a wicked avatar, then by all means cast your vote for the Socialists and the Green, the libertarians and whoever else looks the part at the right time for the right group. It's not like we have to live in this country or anything.... oh, wait.

And lest we forget, we absolutely must fight against gentrification. But in order to make sure the rally is fully prepared, I'll get the flyers from Kinko's, the tee shirts from the Gap and the stickers from Staples. It's gets cold on the picket line, so make sure somebody brings plenty of Starbucks coffee and Chipotle burritos to keep everybody warm. And we've just got to keep the environment in mind, so we'll carpool…. but not everybody fits into my Prius (sure it's a foreign car, but that's not why the economy sucks…is it?), so we should get a couple of SUVs to carry everyone.

So, what's it going to be then, eh?

It used to be that people, especially young people, were aware of what was going down and never hesitated to call "foul" when things weren't right. Now the appearance of being aware has quadrupled in social value, while actually giving-a-damn has gone the way of the dodo.

Somehow, we've all become plastic cutouts with no taste or sense of our own. We concern ourselves with buying the "right" products from the "right" stores and try to agree with the "right" points of view. Meanwhile, back in reality…

Some of us have become that jerk who buys the most expensive bottle of wine (and tells everyone about it) mistakenly thinking that high price equals high quality. Others are morphing into genre-geeks who go out of their way to find obscure movies, books and music-not because they dig it, but solely because it's obscure. Some of us have even become the worst kind of scum, self-righteous zealots who try to force others to adhere to our own twisted rationales."

"Damn, how high was my soap box back then?"

"Well obviously, in the moment, it was infuriating, frustrating, exasperating, and dehumanizing. But posers are posers, and it seemed like nobody was calling anything or anyone out, so I thought I would. And it's not a soap box. It was snarky."

"I have a weird sense of humor, huh?"

"But the look on the faces of the casual bigots when their ignorance was revealed so blatantly…"

"I suppose."

"Do you think the readers are enjoying this?"

"Are you?"

"Well, of course. My philosophy has always been, looking for the light side of every dark situation. At the risk of drowning in the ultimate cliché, life is just too damned short to do otherwise."

"Always?"

"Always."

"Always?"

"Christ, I know this is a one-sided dialogue happening entirely in my head, but is there a frigging echo in here?"

"Well, that's a story there, no?"

"What?"

"My perpetual state of slightly cynical, often Cassandraic optimism."

"I suppose. But that's a heartbreaking story."

"Indeed."

"Heartbreak isn't commonly associated with stories that are light-hearted."

"But this is what the readers want. So, I'll ask straight out, and because it's me asking…"

"Then I'll have to answer."

"That's right."

"Fine. Go ahead and ask."

"Why are you so optimistic?"

HOPE IS HARD TO RESIST

I was seven years old when my Ma was diagnosed with terminal breast cancer. She'd found a sizable, irregularly-shaped, lump in her breast, and tests confirmed that it was cancerous. I didn't know what was going on. I just knew that my Ma and Dad were sad, scared, and worried. My sister and I would sit in blissful ignorance, bouncing on the squishy seats of the waiting rooms of various hospitals and clinics, completely oblivious to the serious conversations from which phrases like "terminal," "hospice," and "get your affairs in order" floated over our heads.

When we got home, my Ma and Dad sat my sister and I down in the living room. Even at that young age, we knew something serious was about to transpire. Ours was a family of laughter and constant conversation. Topics weren't topics so much as chapter markers in an ongoing quadrilogue that only paused for sleep and separation. Sitting on the couch in our 20th floor apartment overlooking Lake Michigan, those few dozen seconds of silence were telling.

I don't remember the exact words or sentences my parents used, but the message was impossible to misunderstand. My Ma was likely going to die.

Of all the emotions, grief isn't something that can be compartmentalized or rationalized. The somewhat cynical adage that death is a part of life is fatuous when the experience is firsthand. While few would question the inconceivability of telling somebody in the throes of grief that they'll get beyond it, or that the emotional, physical, and psychological affliction will pass in a matter of months or even years after the fact, what many don't discuss is that no set time frame for you begin mourning. It can happen before the loss.

Mourning is a procedure, not an event, and it has absolutely no respect for the forward momentum of the temporal flow. Like the Tenth Doctor explained about time, the apprehension and anguish of loss isn't a strict progression of cause and effect. It's a crushing boulder of wibbly-wobbly, timey-wimey.

My Ma was sitting just inches away on the couch. Obviously, I'd seen her innumerous times before. Hell, I'd seen her face literally every day of my young life. But in those moments, it was different.

An understanding set in that she wasn't sick like when I drank spoiled milk. She was sick in a way that forced us to become empiric experts on the nature of mortal impermance.

Family is not meant to be ephemeral. And in my young mind, the possibility and probability were impossibly foreign concepts. As far as I could comprehend, there wasn't a chance that my Ma was going to die. She was already dead.

For the next few weeks, I missed my Ma. She was there just like before. A few more doctor's appointments and less time watching television after dinner, but to me she was gone. After all these years, it's still one of the most bizarre sensations I've ever experienced- being in mourning for someone who still poured the milk over your cereal at breakfast and tucked you in at bedtime every night.

Making the entire situation worse, were the well-wishers. Anytime an adult came to me and spat out empty platitudes, my tiny mind overflowed with rage. I don't know who started the rumor that lazily recycled catchphrases can serve as adequate consolation, but the fact of the matter is that nothing can console.

There is no effective way to reimburse true loss. It is a hole that can never be filled. It is an equation that cannot be solved. Nothing said or done could or can provide comfort, only fleeting distraction.

Grief is an individual experience. It's an emotional state distinctive to every mourner, and unique to every loss. Grief may crash periodically in waves of crushing emotional distress, where times of peace and quiet are suddenly smashed by overwhelming emotion. It might hang over your conscience, like the early morning fog over a rural lake, shrouding your view, stubbornly obscuring the light from piercing through.

There was only one piece of consolation that sank in. Out of all the teachers and neighbors and friends, and people at church, and people at the shops and stores we frequented, only one person said something that actually made a difference. My Dad.

How he kept things together, I have no clue. Even to this day, I'm awestruck and completely baffled by how he was able to get up and get done what needed doing throughout the entire ordeal. I asked him, and his answer embedded in my young mind, and has stayed there ever since.

"Dad, Ma is sick. Why aren't you sad?"

"I am sad. And your mother is sick. But she's sick. As long as she's sick, she's still here. Since she's still here, there are things we have to do, and things we get to do, so let's do them all."

Luckily for my sister and I, my Ma demanded additional tests and diagnosis. She switched docs and specialists when needed. And miraculously, through lots of procedures, treatments, and other major, minor, and medium-sized miracles, she pulled through.

I recognize fully that this isn't something that everyone is able to accomplish. There are millions who lose medical/health battles for a wide variety of reasons. Some of those reasons are tragically preventable, some horrifically inevitable. And I'm fully aware that my family was blessed, lucky, spaghetti-monstered, or whatever term you want to use.

My Ma being here is a gift. The outcome could've been indisputably worse. That I've been able to see, speak, text, or see her any time, any day since then has been something I can't- nor won't- take for granted.

And that's been the outlook applied to every scenario since. My optimism isn't pure. It's tainted by cynicism, Cassandraic ennui, pragmatism, and all the other factors of an alert, observant person living today.

Always knowing that it could be worse isn't blind ignorance to the matter at hand, but a gentle reminder that whatever is happening could be a lot more dire.

The kicker is however, that whatever is happening could also be a lot better than it is. Like the ancient saying goes, it's not over until it's over, and until it's over, I aggressively choose to focus on the latter.

"Since she's still here, there are things we have to do, and things we get to do, so let's do them all."

It's that last bit that really stuck with me. Of course, we have obligations, there are always things that *need* to be done. But the meat of my father's wisdom, what really hit me was the sentiment concentrated in that follow up quip. Obligations are a given, but it's the *things we get to do*, that drove home the point.

BLACK NERD, BLUE BOX

WE MIGHT SEE ANYTHING

"That wasn't really heartbreaking."

"I thought my Ma was going to die."

"But she didn't."

"Just because the circumstances worked out in the end, that doesn't negate the darkness experienced on the way to getting to a favorable end."

"Fair point."

"The primary benefit of hindsight isn't to label memories into superfluous categories like 'good' experiences and 'bad' experiences. Especially since those descriptors are interchangeable depending upon the point of view. The reason why looking back is worthwhile is because it shapes the outlook moving forward. Everything is and isn't, was and wasn't."

"I'm talking like this again?"

"Sure, it sounds like high school-level philosophy, or a cheesy metaphysical slogan that some out-of-touch, suburbanite would use in a flimsy attempt to apply meaning to the meaningless. But am I wrong?"

"No. It's not wrong. Just wish I could phrase it in a less platitudinal fashion."

"This is how I talk."

"Yeah, I know. It's frustratingly authentic."

"Authentic. Yes!"

"What about it?"

"Earlier, I talked about the conflicting, contradictory nature of our society. How the hypocrisy of championing self-delusion and false personas is the bread and butter, so-to-speak, of American culture."

"Right. Like that time in high school, when Mr.…."

"Watch it now."

"What?"

"Don't use real names."

"How would they know if I did? I mean, what are the odds that the people involved will read this?"

"Sliding scale sure. Some of the folks in my past life, are still heavily involved in my current life. Some not so much, but why take the chance?"

"Fine. I'll use fake names. Super fake. Like that time in high school, when…uh, let's call them, Mr. Peanut Butter Sandwich."

"Nicely done."

"So, like I was saying, remember when Mr. Peanut Butter Sandwich asked about nonconformity?"

"That was fantastic!"

"Right?!"

"Mr. Peanut Butter Sandwich had just finished giving a lecture on how social status applies to both quantitative and qualitative categorization."

"Yep, someone can say they're rich, because there's an established baseline of what constitutes average and poor, so it's verifiable. But someone saying they're a go-getter can't validate the claim."

"And then Mr. Peanut Butter Sandwich used nonconformity as an example and asked everyone in class to raise their hands if they felt they were nonconformist, and like ninety percent of the class raised their hands."

"The irony was lost on so many kids!"

"But let's tie it back to one of the principle themes of this book."

"Okay."

"Race doesn't exist, but racists do. However, most people would never claim to be racist."

"Or at best, they'd say something asinine like, they're just a little bit racist."

"That annoys the hell out of me."

"Like, how can you be a little racist?"

"Exactly. It's an either/or proposition. Like how you can't be a little bit pregnant."

"Or a little bit alive."

"Right. So, you have a cripplingly oppressive social system dependent wholly upon superfluous factors, created solely for oppression, but nobody propones the system, but acknowledges that it's an issue."

"Race isn't real, and nobody is a racist, but racism is a massive problem to be addressed."

"Which it is."

"Obviously, so the self-delusion is pervasive to the point that it's the default state."

"Speaking of state, how's Minnesota?"

"What?"

"How's Minnesota?"

"Well, I've been here for a really long time."

"That's not at all what I asked."

"True."

"So…"

"Minneapolis is…"

"Yes?"

"It's different."

"Clearly."

"But I mean, really different."

"I know it's different. By definition, it's not Chicago, so it's different than Chicago."

"In order to adequately explain the differences of Minneapolites, perhaps I should explain Chicagoans?"

"Maybe. But listing differences between two major metropolitan areas in the upper Midwest could be a little boring, a little mundane."

"What if I sprinkle in Doctor Who references?"

"As a way to highlight the culture shock of relocating from Chicago to Minneapolis? Is that something I can do?"

"Of course. I am a nerd, after all."

BLACK NERD, BLUE BOX

WHERE I'M FROM

In the woefully underrated, Doctor Who movie (the one made for television, that gave us the equally underrated, and incredibly brief, televised tenure, of Paul McGann's Eighth Doctor) there's a moment when the Eighth Doctor and Grace Holloway (played by the stupendously charismatic Daphne Ashbrook), are chatting about Gallifrey.

Eight describes laying in the grass with his father watching a brilliant meteor storm, in which dancing lights flashed across the sky, dancing with brilliance. It's kind of a cheesy line by itself, but in context- especially given the amazing performances of McGann and Ashbrook- the scene always strikes a painfully relatable, emotional chord.

I was born and raised in Chicago, Illinois. And while my hometown of Chicago isn't exactly some unknown municipality that only a few people have heard of, even with a well-above-average level of international name recognition, there are more than a few aspects of Chicago life that aren't really that well known outside of us schmooeys.

Take "schmooey" for example. That's old neighborhood slang for what most others might refer to as a "Chicagoan." It's very flexible actually, and can be used as a warm greeting, a neutral identifier, as well as a cold insult- often in the same sentence, even when referencing the same person. For example:

"So that f**king schmooey that I thought was a real stand up schmooey turned out to be a sneaky schmooey f**k."

It sounds nutty, I know, and when two schmooeys happen to run into each other outside of Chicago, the expressions of those witnessing their conversation are not at all unlike that puzzled look Donna gives the Tenth Doctor when he speaks Judoon (in the fantastic episode, The Stolen Earth).

I didn't fully appreciate it at the time, but my neighborhood stomping grounds were the real-life version of the idealized American, major metropolitan community. It allowed and accepted everyone to be whoever, and dress however, they wanted.

You know how some people get annoyed when someone says they prefer to judge people based on who they are rather than their skin color? I spent my formative years fully immersed among the latter.

In Hyde Park, if you were on the level, everyone you encountered treated you well. It was, and is, one of the most genuinely diverse neighborhoods in the country. What you looked like was worthless. Who you were was all that really mattered.

And although it's not literally in the center of the city geographically, with Lake Shore Drive and major public transportation routes running through it (and being home to numerous, nationally recognized attractions) it felt like the it epicenter of not just Chicago, but the known universe as well.

It took years before I realized my neighborhood was an anomaly- both compared to other communities in Chicago, as well as neighborhoods across the country. My blissful obliviousness was maintained due in no small part to my exceptionally patient, and remarkably adventurous parents.

It never struck me as odd that we would regularly traverse a massive segment of the Chicagoland area for food, entertainment, and other needs that *could* have been acquired closer to home. In fact, it was so expectedly obvious that I never even thought to question the practice.

Why wouldn't we go to Lulu's on Taylor street? Their Chicago dogs and cheese fries are the best in the city. Let's hit up Mama Tish (also on Taylor street) for Italian ice and pick up birthday presents at Cook Brothers on North and Kostner. Of course, we'll head way north to Caputo's on Harlem and Grand for groceries. Their prices are crazy low, and the deserts are insanely delicious. We grabbed Rib tips and fries from Uptown Pizza & BBQ on Wilson, steaks from Matteson's on 81st. We went to the beach near Evanston and fed seagulls on the Southshore.

On top of this, both my sister and I went to schools all over the place. Forty-five minute and even hour-long school bus rides were not uncommon before I reached high school. And speaking of high school, I was still a good half-hour or more away via car, depending on how late I was running that morning.

But even beyond the weekend excursions, the extracurricular activities, and Monday through Friday academic obligations, my parents were absolutely incredible at allowing our interests- no matter how flighty- to flourish unfettered.

When I said I thought it might be cool to go camping, my parents enrolled me in a Cub Scout troop, and found reasonably priced wilderness accessories. When my interests in Star Trek shifted towards the starships, we spent hours at the Henry Crown Space Center, and launching water rockets. When I got into comic books, they drove me to comic shops, and would patiently let me explore any collectible and memorabilia stores we came across.

I've met many people over the years who had contentious, strained, abusive, and/or otherwise negative relationships with their folks. I was definitely lucky. That's not to say that we always got along. I wasn't a bad kid per se, but I was still a kid. And like every kid ever born anywhere, I was prone to mischief and backtalk, and cutting up and goofing off. And my parents weren't slow when it came to discipline. But even when I was getting (rightfully) punished for troublemaking, it was obvious even then that the reprimand was being handed down out of love.

I'm not flaunting our familial contentment. Even then, I was extremely aware of just how fortunate my sister and I were. I want you to have context.

My comparatively unique family from a verifiably unique neighborhood was an example of a sort of quintessential Chicagoan mindset. Even though the third largest city in the couched in the Midwest, less than a day's drive from numerous other midwestern cities, Chicago was distinctive.

A teacher once pointed to Chicago on a map of the US and said, "this is Chicago." They then pointed to the rest of the map, "And this doesn't matter. Because this is Chicago." I didn't learn much geography that day, but I got a crystal-clear insight into Chicago pride. In the interest of brevity, here's a short list of what makes Chicagoans well, Chicagoans:

NOT BEING FROM NEW YORK

A popular fan theory is that the TARDIS sends the Doctor wherever the Doctor is most needed. While the Doctor has been to NYC numerous times to help save those Big Appletinis, Chicagoans have rarely needed the help of the greatest Gallifreyan. If there's one thing schmooeys can do, it's fend for themselves. We survived a real fire started by a fictious cow, that destroyed the city. We can handle a couple of aliens.

Could you imagine a Dalek trying to make its way down LSD during rush hour? With the nonstop, 24/7 crowds, a Weeping Angel would be frozen forever if it ever came to the Mag Mile. And Harold Saxon wouldn't have even made it on the ballot, before the Machine would've ground him up and spit him out.

Schmooeys love being from Chicago, and we also love Not being from New York. This is less about comparing quality of life, and more about key differences in (junk) food. NYC pizza limp and flaccid. Chicago pizza is thick and delicious. Chicago dogs are a taste explosion. NYC hot dogs come with soggy sauerkraut, and questionable storage methods."

Speaking of which, this hyper intense love of our hometown makes us…

AGGRESSIVELY TERRITORIAL

Schmooeys love to travel. We mostly like traveling for the same reason other people do, but we especially love finding other people abroad who claim to be from Chicago and then pointing out that Evanston, Skokie, Dalton, Deerfield, Oak Park, Northlake and dozens of other Chicagoland suburbs are NOT Chicago.

We actually love calling out this differentiation so much, it becomes a tradition. It's expected that when sharing stories upon our return home, that at least one to four conversations goes like this:

"I was out at dis one bar out west, California like. Just sipping a whiskey-gingers when this broad comes ova. I buys her a bottle of 312 and we gets to talkin'. Chick says she's from Chicago. I'm like cool, me too what part ya from? She goes, Zion. I'm like Zion? That ain't Chicago sweetie. Can ya believe dat? Trying to pass off Zion as Chicago. I left her ass at the bar…"

Those aren't typos by the way. They're a phonetic representation of…

DA DIALECT

We don't go to Jewel, we go to "da Jewels." See the people at the park? Nope, we see the "peoples". Weekend plans? We went to "da movies." The Chicago dialect (made famous by the Saturday Night Live's Billy Goats Grill and Super Fans sketches) isn't as prevalent as it may seem, but it's real.

It's not about bad grammar and questionable pronunciation, so much as it's about speaking fast and low out of the side of your mouth. It's almost another language. Actually, when you sprinkle in the local slang, it pretty much is another language. Gallifreyan may be ridiculously challenging to decipher- what with its alphabet based on circles and arcs- but da Dialect mixed with local colloquialisms, can be just as, if not more so, perplexing.

But Chicago culture isn't just oddly phrased idioms and dangerously passionate, geography-based pride. Like many American cities, we have some painfully basic, unquestionably middlebrow interests as well. We just blow it out to extremes. For example, consider our love of…

THE CUBS

Imagine the Great Time War, but with a lot more cargo shorts, backwards caps, and an alarmingly large number of people, proudly referring to themselves as Trixie or Chad as they engage in odd rituals like unironic chest bumps, group high fives, and trying to get a street-level selfie with a 135-foot-tall sign.

Chicagoans love their sports teams, and perhaps none more than the boys in blue who rock the "friendly confines." Diehard fans are easily identifiable by their licensed gear, and well-worn look that comes with heartbreak and cheap beer.

The Crosstown Classic game between the Cubs and the White Sox is a slightly less violent Civil War. Yes, the Sox were the first to win a World Series in the 21st Century, but the biggest celebration of grown men being paid millions of dollars to play a child's sport happened eleven years later, at the corner of Addison and Clark.

The rivalry between the Cubs and the Sox doesn't really make sense. Both teams are from the same city, but they play in different parts of that city, and aren't even in the same league. But like the American political spectrum, you must choose a side.

And speaking of politics…

THE "MACHINE"

Aside from Ancient Rome perhaps, no other city has mastered the art of political wheeling and dealing to the extent of Chicago's Machine.

The simple premise, do for me and I'll do for you, is so engrained in the underlying fabric of Chicago culture, that we're often surprised when we meet people who treat politics and government as if it's not a for-profit entity.

It may be unethical, it's definitely questionable, and often at times it can be downright corrupt, but it's manageable and efficient. I mean, what does everyone else operate on? Ideals? No thank you.

Say you're meeting with a political figure- not necessarily a full-on elected official, but someone with just enough authority to help get something accomplished. If they say no because they don't see how it benefits their office, you can reason with them. Idealism though? They say "no, because I talked to god" and that's the end of conversation.

It takes a lot of smart people to keep the machine running. Sometimes- okay, fairly often- bad things happen, but it's not out of sheer malevolence (well, politically speaking. Police brutality and racism is a whole other monster), but as we learned from the Third Doctor, superior intelligence senseless brutality don't go together.

BLACK NERD, BLUE BOX

NOTHING IS INEXPLICABLE

"What the hell?"

"What?"

"I was looking for insights into Chicago culture as a comparative base against which to highlight the differences between my hometown and Minneapolis."

"And?"

"And instead, what started as an insightful description of the neighborhood, and how it may have influenced my outlook, devolved into one of those silly listicle pieces you find on boring websites!"

"Not all listicles are boring."

"Don't be snarky."

"I'm not being snarky."

"A listicle in the middle of a memoir?"

"It's *my* memoir and I like listicles. Plus, I think it makes for a nice break considering how heavy the other stories have been and will be moving forward."

"I don't have to focus on the heavy content though. It's not as though my entire life has been nothing but sad and negative experiences."

"But that's just it, isn't it?"

"What?"

"Experiences aren't sad and negative. Experiences aren't happy and positive. Once they've transitioned from present event to past recollection, then they're just experiences. They occurred, and depending on the context through which they're viewed, they're either positive, negative, both, and/or neither."

"That's a bit of a privileged point of view though, isn't it?"

"How so?"

"I mean, I've read other memoirs and autobiographies. Some of them- many of them- were truly gut wrenching. To say that they're devoid of connotation is at the very best, insensitive, and at worse, dismissive of the feelings of the people who went through them."

"That's a solid point, but I'm not referring to experiences in the universal sense. I'm talking specifically in the context of this collection."

"Oh."

"Yeah. Oh."

"That kind of clarity would've been helpful."

"That's why I provided it."

"See. Snarky."

"I know I'm a bit snarky. But I'm busting my chops, and literally baring my soul. I'm not one to play my cards out in the open. I don't let people in without extensive, massive amounts of time and shared interactions to assure me that someone besides myself can be trusted."

"But this is a book."

"That it is."

"What I mean to say is that, by putting myself in the pages of the book, literally condensing your lived experiences into consumable portions, laid out in a semi-narrative fashion, I'm going in the completely opposite direction."

"Am I though? I mean, this is what certain kinds of introverts do well. It's like hiding in plain sight. I provide a ton of stories and content, but this is an introduction to a person, a walk-through, carefully aggregated tour of a life lived. The reader will know of me, and know details about me, but would they really say that they knew…me?"

"That's kind of clever."

"Thank you."

"No, really. It's sort of a literary version of that old business trick. When surrounded by strangers, at a party, conference, or networking event, to avoid having to open up too much about yourself, you instead ask questions, and keep the other person talking about themselves."

"Exactly."

"But a book isn't a conversation."

"Technically, neither is this."

"Touché."

"So, what do I want people to take away from this?"

"Different people will (hopefully) have different reactions, and definitely have different takeaways. If it's a young black kid, whose interests lie way outside the mainstream, acceptable norms of what young black kids are "supposed" to be into, then for them, this is a message of hope."

"Hope?"

"That there's nothing wrong with digging what they dig. As long as it doesn't hurt anybody else, or themselves, then they should go for it.

"And if it's someone who's the opposite? Someone who is the epitome of the status quo?"

"Like some popular white kid, who has a ton of friends, and is really into all the stuff they're supposed to be really into?

"Then this is a humanizing introduction to someone unlike themselves, and hopefully when they're interacting out in the real world with people who are unlike themselves, they'll remember this book, and treat that person, like a person worthy of courtesy and respect, instead of an oddball to ridicule."

"Well, let's get into it then. Let's show the reader who I really am."

"The thing is though that my reluctance to do that isn't without merit."

"Oh, it's definitely a legit concern. With my other endeavors, if someone hates it, we can still get along."

"I mean, I do want people to like my fictional work, and my music, and my television shows, and the panels I'm on at geeky conventions."

"Well of course, but for example, if someone hates my Afrofuturism novels, I can kind of pass off their disinterest to other factors. Maybe the story didn't grab them, or they weren't a fan of the character arcs, or the ending, or the whatever."

"But with this. If they hate this, what they're saying is that they hate me."

"Yeah, but if it's not scary, what's the point?"

"It's like visiting Paris. You can't just read, or I suppose in this case, write the guidebook. You've got to throw yourself in."

"Ninth Doctor?"

"Of course. Nine is ridiculously underrated."

"It would be pretty dull if I didn't put myself out there, wouldn't it?"

"Painfully so."

"But now I've got to go back and redo it, so it's more linear. Sort of I was there, now I'm here."

"That might be the most concise way to bet between two points, but it's definitely not the most interesting way to go."

"Third Doctor."

"Also ridiculously underrated."

"I'm convinced."

"Well, of course I am. I convinced me."

"Now who's the snarky one?"

"Still."

"Does that mean then, that this one-sided, wholly internal dialogue is no longer necessary?"

"Probably wasn't all that necessary to begin with."

"Right on. From here on out, I'll just let the recollections speak for themselves?"

"Sounds groovy to me."

"Groovy."

BLACK NERD, BLUE BOX

YOUR NATURAL HORRID SELF

When the nineties started, I was 5'10" tall, with a size twelve shoe, and a physique lanky enough to fit through a basketball hoop. I was even taller than a bunch of my teachers. My sartorial choices reflected my interests, and my interests weren't exactly at the top of the popularity pyramid.

Gangsta rap had just begun its saturation of pop culture. While most kids were rocking baggy tees, tracksuits, and ginormous jeans, my style was present day Grunge Rock meets Post-War hipster, with a heavy dose of Sixties Psychedelia.

It wasn't MTV or BET. It was WTF.

My go-to outfit was a tie-dyed tee and shredded jeans as a base. Then I'd either tie a plaid shirt around my waist, or wear it open, and half tucked. I'd top off the look with a beanie, Doc Martens, and way too many pieces of cheap, pewter jewelry. While many Black boys were emulating the asymmetrical fade that Tupac rocked in the film Juice, my hairstyle was closer to Frederick Douglas with a hangover.

"Let me catch you playing that devil stuff again. I swear! I'll kick you in mouth and break your teeth. Punk ass white boy nerd."

He held my cassette tape just out of reach. For a moment I thought he was going to break it. He'd already thrown me to the ground and punched me in the face. Even though my eye hurt, I was more concerned about saving my music than potentially having to hide a shiner.

The "devil stuff" that had triggered this latest round of beatings was Kickstart My Heart, by Motley Crue, which he had heard blasting from my headphones, in a rare moment of carelessness. Silly me. I thought I was so clever. Thought I'd been careful.

The night before, I'd taken my Batman soundtrack cassette (the Danny Elfman score, not the collection of woefully underrated Prince tunes) and put scotch tape over the tabs. It was an old hack that enabled you to record over store bought tapes.

I'd been getting really into the local rock music station, The Loop. And had taped a bunch of music that at the time, I thought was the hardest, most extreme rock music ever created.

Looking back, yeah, it's pretty funny. I mean, here's this little, cappuccino-colored kid with crazy hair, thinking he's the ultimate rebel because he idolized a bunch of fellas in makeup and spandex singing about parties, cars, and girls. But at the time, the combination of distorted guitars and tenor vocals were a subversive anti-establishment soundtrack.

Motley Crue's Kickstart My Heart was one of my favorite tunes, mostly because there's a line in the bridge where Vince Neil says the word, "ass" …twice!

I was well aware at this point of how dangerous my tastes could be. Sure, the late eighties/early nineties were all about authenticity, but I'd learned the hard way, that the philosophy of *keeping it real* didn't extend to black kids who liked hair metal.

But for 1 moment, the Batman soundtrack deception kept me safe. My on again-off again tormentor, Tyrannosaurus (not his real name), saw me carrying the tape case, and let me go. But when I cranked up the Crue, and he overheard something more suitable for headbanging and pogoing, than head-bopping and breakdancing, blaring from my headphones, he unleashed hell.

He menacingly held my poorly hidden audio indulgence in his fist. There was a look of twisted enjoyment smeared across his young face. He relished in these moments of uncontested dominance. I was six inches taller, and a good fifteen pounds heavier, but I was as much a nerd as he was a bully and kicking around someone so much physically larger clearly gave him an insatiable power rush.

"Why do you listen to this devil stuff?" he smirked,

"I don't know. I just, like it." I whimpered, trying desperately to hold back the tears aggressively welling up in my sore eyes.

"This is that devil stuff those white boys on TV listen to. Why you trying to be white? You hate black people or something? Why don't you keep it real?"

"I ain't trying to be white, I just like it."

"White boy, devil stuff." Tyrannosaurus spat. He threw my tape on the ground and stomped on it.

You know how in teen movies from the eighties, where in the third act, the nerd stands up to the bully, and be the sheer act of defiance, the bully concedes, and sometimes even apologizes?

That was not this moment.

"What the hell!" I screamed. To both of our surprise, I jumped to my feet and pushed him, "It took me an hour to make that!"

Because of our physical differences, my shove sent him stumbling backwards. Then the realization set in. There kids who fight, and kids who don't fight. I was not a kid who fights.

He got back to his feet and kicked me in the stomach. I crumpled to the ground and curled into a ball to try and lessen the pain and damage of his blows. The outpouring of epithets was impressive for a kid his age. He unleashed a typhoon of verbal belligerence, calling into question my intelligence and masculinity with all manner of homophobic and ableist slurs.

It felt like hours passed as he delivered his tortuous punishment. I know he was embarrassed. The geeky kid pushed him down. It was a violation of the natural law of the playground.

I pulled myself to my feet, trying in vain to ignore the other kids who'd been watching. Their voyeuristic silence was the same as my classmates' years earlier, when my teacher embarrassed me for wearing my homemade, Doctor Who tee shirt.

To them, it was just another episode of the kick the crap out of the nerd show. A long running series that had been going on for so long, it wasn't even worth talking about afterwards. Taylor says, wears, or does something nerdy. Tyrannosaurus beats him up. They'd seen the show before. But nobody cared enough to even consider it could be or should be changed.

To me however, this was the final straw. No, there wasn't an awesome moment where I waited until Tyrannosaurus' back was turned, and pounced on him, delivering some semi-justifiable retribution for years of neighborhood torment.

Instead, as Tyrannosaurus walked away laughing, one of the older kids, who hung out by the benches just outside the playground area, came over and helped me straighten my jacket.

"Hey man, you okay?"

"What? Um, yeah I guess."

"What's up with that dude?"

"He doesn't like my music."

The older kid picked up the cracked cassette and handed it to me. It was completely ruined. No amount of scotch tape was going to be able to make it playable.

"Batman? He kicked you ass over Batman?"

"No. I recorded over it. I was listening to…"

I stopped mid-sentence. I'd just survived my regularly scheduled assault. I was definitely not looking for a back-to-back, beatdown.

"What? What were you listening to?"

"Motley Crue."

"Really? That's cool."

I was dumbfounded. The things I was interested in had been called a lot of things- the vast majority of which I'd never repeat- but cool was definitely not one of them.

"You think Motley Crue is cool?"

"I mean," older kid began as he dusted off my jacket, "I think it' cool that you were hiding it on that Batman tape. Crue is all right, but I think that hair metal stuff is a little cheesy. You know Bad Brains?"

"What's Bad Brains?"

The older kid smirked, reached in his pocket and gave me one of those aftermarket blank tapes. A swatch of masking tape ran across the top, on which song titles were scrawled in sloppy, blue ink.

"Bad Brains is way cooler than hair metal."

"Thanks."

"Don't thank me. Just listen to it."

The older kid nodded and walked back across the playground. I threw the crushed remnants of my Batman/Motley Crue tape in the trash, and popped my newly acquired, hand-labeled, cassette into my Walkman and pressed play.

The opening chords of Sailin' On blasted through my headphones. Before the song ended just under two minutes later, I was a total convert. No more Motely Crue, no more hair metal. I even neglected my standard favorites like Jimi Hendrix, The Beatles, and jazz.

A few days later the older kid told me that the tape was a dubbed copy of Bad Brains' self-titled EP, aka The Yellow Tape. Completely blew my mind. I'd never heard anything so raw and passionate, yet at the same time musically proficient and complex.

A little while later I got a copy of Quickness, the newest (at the time) Bad Brains record. The music was amazing, but even more mind-blowing was that the photo of the band on the cover. This wasn't "white boy devil stuff." This was four black guys with beards, long dreads and plaid shirts.

The vindication was nice, but I already knew that the music I dug- and all music in general- wasn't beholden to one racial group or another. What was awesome was that I could exploit the racial-based ignorance of Tyrannosaurus and the other bullies.

I could leave the cassette tapes out on the lunch table, or read the liner notes openly on the school bus, and kids would stare, but as long as I kept the music down, all they saw was Black guys on the cover, and because of their ridiculous, erroneous beliefs that rock was "white" and "pop" was Black, they left me alone.

And the key word there is alone. I was alone, but not lonely. And as grammar school creeped into middle school, high school and beyond, the notion of following the trend faded from popularity, and digging what you dug became the new hip.

BLACK NERD, BLUE BOX

JELLY BABY

"I though the one-sided dialogue was over."

"I hope it never ends."

"Why?"

"Because that means I'm dead, or at the very least, not longer compelled or engaged enough to the point that my endeavors warrant a discussion."

"I guess that's true. I definitely can't get enough."

"It's never be enough."

"I mean, I can't get enough."

"It was never going to be enough."

"Even if there's no great weeping eye is in the sky watching down on us as we eat, laugh, sleep, and dream. There's promise of a paradise after death in exchange for a life free from only the most desirable of sins and reluctant of hearts."

"I'm a bit young to be worried about legacy."

"Not legacy in the posthumous sense. The concurrent and ongoing interests ignited by the past and concurrent achievements- or lack thereof."

"When I was a young man, I never felt very young."

"I remember crushing on groovy dames way back before I could read books that didn't contain meticulously illustrated pictures, and slightly moralistic plots involving anthropomorphized mammals in brightly colored shirts."

"I've been growing up ever since."

"The last time I was truly happy, I was far too young to appreciate the fact that this was probably the last time that I'd be truly happy."

"Yeah, but happiness is a recreational drug, and I am all about the notion that vices should be indulged and consumed in moderation."

"Recreation, procreation, desecration, in a week no one cares, in a month no one remembers."

"No one?"

"I remember."

"So, share it subversively. Mask it like a scented candle covering the stench of a dingy apartment."

"Like vanilla."

"Oh, hell yeah, vanilla."

"I love that scent."

"I dig it too!"

"Vanilla is the smell of fresh and new, of clean and clarity, of peace and chill."

"Okay, that's enough with the new agey suburbanite silliness. Let's get squishy personal."

"What constitutes, squishy personal?"

"Like coming-of-age stuff."

"Like my first date?"

"No, like the first desire."

"Ooh, that could be groovy."

"Very groovy. But divulging those kinds of details is bad form. At the very least, it's like kiss & tell, and that's not something I'm particularly keen on."

"So instead of telling what happened, maybe I should play it- like a bass solo."

"How am I going to play a memory? Especially a memory that I'm expressing via the written word?"

"The same way I play a solo without writing the notation first, or dance to a song you've never heard before, it's like eating before you get hungry, dig?"

"I can dig it…"

BLACK NERD, BLUE BOX

LOVE IS ALWAYS WISE

I learned so much about nothing during the three years in which we were "together," except for why the hell everything was such a huge issue. There was no casual interest. It was all of nothing, calm or chaos. It was the way it had to be in the last breaths of summer, just steps away from high school.

I can't remember her name, so I'll refer to her as Vanilla Bean. I don't know if Vanilla Bean liked strawberry or chocolate flavored milk shakes. I don't know whether it was artists that I completely respected or absolutely loathed with all the anti-celebrity loathing an eighth-grader could muster, that performed Vanilla Bean's favorite music.

I kind of remember Vanilla Bean's hair, and I can vaguely, picture her chipped nail polish. What's important however, what's forever and legendary, and will keep her permanently engrained in my memory until either my mind or my body dies, was a single feeling from a moment, all of which started as an accidental night.

It's not a date without something to do. When you're twelve years old on a Friday night and the weatherman says it's below zero and you happen to live in Chicago, there isn't much to do.

You could stay home listening to Nirvana records while watching the network television programs, you could do chores, or you could do homework. That's pretty much it. We thought we would defy the odds. We decided to get up, get dressed, and go all the way downtown, and see a movie.

An hour later we found ourselves stranded on the Magnificent Mile having grossly underestimated the amount of cash needed to catch an opening night show, but the night was still young, so we share a meal at McDonald's, wander around the mall until security realizes that though we do look a lot like all the other gum-chewing, cigarette holding schmucks on MTV, we most likely were not.

Politely, but not so polite as to undermine their authority, the security officers made it clear that we needed to start shopping or start leaving.

"Guess it's time to go." Vanilla Bean smiles.

"Go where?" I smile back.

"Outside."

"Too cold outside."

"We've got coats."

"Guess you're right."

Zipped up, bundled up, wrapped in tightly, winds cutting through layer upon layer upon layer of cotton, wool and nylon. I can't feel anything except her shoulders nuzzled into my side.

Is this romance or idiocy?

Standing in an alley near a large vent for heat, waiting for our respective rides and everybody's late. Find myself standing at the payphone, sharing a booth while we shiver in tandem, scrunched up against the plexiglass sides of the booth walls.

Complaining about the myriad of ways that this phone booth is nowhere near as cool as the TARDIS, but mostly repeating variations of the same "joke" about how American phone booths are smaller on the inside. We drop a quarter in the slot to make the calls and there's bad news for both on the other end.

"It's going to be a while."

I hang up the phone and we shift positions. The shared booth is still uncomfortable, still foggy. She's standing in front of me, leaned against me, pressed against me. We pass the time with a saccharinely cheesy game of one-upsmanship.

"I like it here."

"I love it here."

"I could sleep here."

"I could die here."

A knock on the phonebooth door disrupts the game. Guy outside is annoyed because he has the audacity to want to use the phonebooth to make a phone call, rather than watch us engage in primary school rituals of nerdy courtship.

We're back outside again. We head to the alley way between the buildings where the guys who pulled the shortest straws are working on a Friday evening outside in February.

Commotion in motion, they're loading and unloading, yelling and resting, smoking and laughing, getting done what needs doing. They're wringing and rubbing hands, expelling breaths with only slightly more heat than the outside wind.

It's a sea of nametags stitched across chests. But that tall, broad-shouldered guy? His name isn't written in a style like the other guys. It's bigger with different colors. He must be a boss.

"What are you two kids doing over there?" boss shouted at us.

"What are *you* doing over there?" Vanilla Bean shouted back.

"Friggin' kids." Boss shook his head.

"I know, right!" I chimed in.

Boss leaves us alone. Must be lunch because all of the unfortunate guys who drew the shorter of the straws are all filing back inside the big building from which they're loading and unloading, packing and swearing, running and carrying.

It's just the two of us. Noses running, hands shaking. It's dark out, but the sky is clear for a city night. You can see the clouds against the black, purple, black of the sky. Facing each other, her head down, I can smell her shampoo. I don't remember the brand, but I absolutely remember the scent.

Vanilla.

In the future, if the pulp sci-fi writers are correct, and our cities are encased in a massive cloche domes, stretching miles into the heavens, then the artificial atmosphere around the globe, should be augmented by a thick ozone of fresh vanilla.

But seriously, if I die with a clean slate and unburdened soul, then my heaven will be forever autumn in the city and the air will be heavy with the most intensely rich, fresh vanilla scents available in this world and the next.

She looks up. Her eyes are honey brown, or maybe burnt cinnamon. Or perhaps they were as bright as amber, or as dark as hickory. My own eyes are walnut with flecks of umber, and I recall her saying that our eyes were the same? Or was she saying that our eye colors were the exact opposite?

A moment passes but we missed it.

She buries her head into my neck and shivers away. Her nose is ice against my jugular. We're standing there, just as we were moments ago. Her head rest on my shoulder. A raging silence floods the streets, drenching the entirety of downtown.

Michigan Avenue is literally a hop, skip, and jump away, but all the cabs, buses, commuters, cops, tourists and loclas who are honking and screaming and screeching and ducking and running find their overture of noise muted, blocked out entirely in our bubble of cold noses, and vanilla scents.

Here is where the problems began.

As I've mentioned before, I was a cappuccino colored, tie-dyed schmooey who towered over some of the teachers, but was skinny enough to fit through the hoop of a basketball net. Vanilla Bean was nearly as tall and twice as brash. My adolescent angel was a foul-mouthed, fast-talking masterpiece with a devilish eyelash that kept you guessing. Together we were like Bonnie and Clyde, but without bank robberies, high-powered firearms, or cop-killing.

Our togetherness fueled the fires of juvenile cruelty that were stoked beneath us by the under-aged, under-grown jerks we called classmates. In protest, we ignored everything and everyone except for our tight circle of friends, the select few who existed on the outskirts of the strict policies and guidelines of the elementary school code of coolness and popularity.

Even our buddies were opposed to us at first, but after a couple of well-placed middle finger flips and slightly excessive, PG-rated displays of public affection, we were all copasetic.

Eighth grade graduation came, and it was over. As quickly as it came, it was gone. Like the last patch of snow on the first day of a sunny-day in spring, the we melted and vaporized, floating away into the next season without a single shred of evidence that we'd even been there before in the first place. Outside the school, mortarboard bumping mortarboard, we stood there taking in the final hug. Our smiling faces were just flimsy masks hiding the irrevocably cracked pottery of our young infatuation.

THE TEA IS GETTING COLD

"That was kind of sweet."

"Not too confusing, was it?"

"I don't think so."

"No more or less than anything else I've written about so far."

"So, what happened next?"

"With her?"

"Not necessarily, but like other girlfriends?"

"I'm not doing that."

"Alone again?"

"Sometimes. And sometimes not. The world is cyclical. The beginning will be the end eventually as will the one after the one before it."

"Christ, I can't believe I actually talk like that."

"Well yeah, I do."

"Okay, well then, if I won't talk about other romantic, non-platonic relationships, then maybe talk about break ups."

"No. The book would be too long."

"That's a little harsh, no?"

"Not really, I mean. I was, and am, a nerd."

"Okay then, what about one major breakup story to balance out the sweetness of the previous?"

"Not for a full memoir. How about right here?"

"Groovy."

"Okay then, dig on this. A fake smile may make friends faster than a genuine scowl, but the truth in feeling will always conquer the hoax."

"Go on."

"In other words, I didn't know that this is how it would end."

"I never do."

"As a child I was picked on mercilessly, as a young man I was expected to accomplish more than I could. Throughout all of the usual boring, sometimes permanently scarring garbage that accompanies childhood, I was told by everyone and anyone that if I was honest nothing could go wrong."

"Because real men don't lie."

"As opposed to make believe ones?"

"Am I telling this or what?"

"My bad."

"Anyway, I'd opened up honestly and it resulted in nothingness. Existence has a dark sense of humor."

"Being a real man can be hard when you haven't finished growing but it's a lot harder when you have."

"No more high school. I was done. I had nothing to look forward to but more school, more work, and eventually death. In the meantime, it was time to take advantage of the little bit of notoriety I was able to scrap together from having been in a band."

"That's kind of cool!"

"Not really. While I was, trying to "make it," everyone else was growing up. Being a musician is cool when you're in your teens. In your twenties though…"

"It's still kind of cool."

"Not as cool as being pre-med, or landing an entry-level gig, with top shelf perks."

"Still kind of cool though."

"Moving on."

"Name?"

"Five String Active Bass with J-Style Pickups."

"That's a bit long."

"Five String Bass?"

"Perfect."

"Any way I asked her out. She said yes. One date, then another date, then it's pick up Five String Bass from work, meet Five String Bass for coffee, and finally let's grab a bite at this fancy joint."

"Sounds like it was going well."

"Then on our fifth date..."

"What?"

"She told me she didn't date Black guys."

"WHAT!!!"

"Sort of. I'm paraphrasing a bit. She didn't use the phrase, *black guys*."

"What word did she use?"

"Starts with N, rhymes with, that was the last effing time I was going out with her."

"Why'd she wait until so many dates though?"

"Said she didn't want to seem racist."

"People are ridiculous."

"Hey, that's a smooth segue."

"Is it."

"Yep. Dig this. Ahem, and speaking of ridiculous people being racists…"

BLACK NERD, BLUE BOX

PUDDING BRAINS

When I moved to the Twin Cities, my first gig as a television producer was launching a talk show for a local network. We'd spent months in preproduction (the time in which everything is worked out, from booking guests, to recording video segments, and fine tuning every aspect of the show), and I'd gotten to know the rest of the producers, associate producers, camera operators, on-air talent, and executives, and they'd gotten to know me.

Or at least that's what I thought.

I'd just moved up to the Twin Cities from Chicago and was looking forward to stepping up into a network gig as a producer, launching my own program. The production team had a wide spectrum of experience. Some were like me, and had spent years in the industry, others were brand new. For our boss, the executive producer, it was their first time as a showrunner.

They were incredibly talented though. Possessing the kind of natural talent that makes you believe in divinity; our EP possessed a shockingly astute knack for every element of production.

They were three steps ahead when it came to planning and scheduling, and like all great producers, there wasn't a problem or issue they couldn't fix with some creative- often last minute- solutions that seamlessly buoyed the production.

I was taken completely by surprise when after months of long hours working closely together, getting to know each other in the studio, office, and after work at happy hours, my EP asked me rap in front of the entire company at the launch party.

Look, I have nothing against rap. And just like anyone else who holds truly eclectic and varied musical tastes, I enjoy a lot of rap songs, albums, and artists.

But my tastes lie primarily within jazz, rock, country, and blues. A wide variety of music flowed from my desk in the production office, and of the dozens of songs played daily over the months leading to the launch party, maybe two or three were rap. The music guests I'd booked showed my tastes were closer to Chicago in the 40s or Seattle in the 90s, as opposed to New York in the 80s.

So, my EP knew that I wasn't a rapper, yet they still decided to put me on the spot. The music player had stopped about two-thirds of the way through the party, and in the awkward silence, punctuated by polite, laughter that accompanies these types of minor technical issues in social settings, my EP broke the ice by saying: *"Taylor, you should rap! You're Black. Rap for us!"*

There was an awkward pause that in reality lasted maybe seven seconds but felt like a few days. Mercifully, someone was able to get the music going again, and the party resumed, but that moment understandably, and irreparably tarnished my relationship with the EP for the remainder of my time on the show.

I'm certain she was ignorant in the truest sense of the word, in that she truly was unaware of the underlying, offensive implications of what she'd said. She almost certainly thought that she was just being playfully cordial and making that request/demand (in front of the entire cast, crew, and other network employees) was nothing more than a jovial ribbing.

Yes, a critical part of our evolution as a species was the development of presumptive shortcuts. But those presumptive shortcuts weren't meant to be used as a blanket. Broad generalities do nothing more than perpetuate stereotyping and monolithic thought.

And yes, rap is associated with Black people- we originated the artform after all. And yes, it's not hard to find a Black person that's familiar and/or a fan of an entire, multi-artist discography of rap songs. But just as not every white person is an Appalachian stereotype with incestuous desires, or woefully inept when it comes to dressing or dancing well, not every Black person is a rapper, nor wants to be.

I wish I could tell you that this was the only instance in the entertainment industry in which something like this occurred. That is not at all the case.

Thankfully, compared to stories of blatant bigotry that I've heard from friends in other fields, they tend to be relatively minor slights. I've never been fired because my hair wasn't "professional." I've never been passed over for promotions or excluded from extracurricular activities based solely on my melanin content. But microaggressions are still aggressions.

Because of the never-ending onslaught of various media formats, we're surrounded by both positive and negative stereotypes every moment. We don't have to retain those depictions. In fact, after a certain age, you should know better than to put too much into what you see online and on-air.

Implicit bias is real sure, but it's not an excuse. Just as every human has cancerous cells throughout their entire life, doesn't necessarily mean that you have a form of cancer, or that you'll contract a form of cancer. All it really means is that by nature of being a human, you possess certain traits.

In that same vein, while you do possess implicit biases, that alone isn't indicative of explicit prejudicial outlooks or deliberately offensive behaviors.

Possessing certain physical characteristics make it more likely that certain benefits, advantages, atrocities, and disadvantages will befall you. Beyond that, everything-and everyone- has exceptions.

Stereotypes aren't ignorant because they're false, so much as because they're wildly inaccurate, woefully incomplete, and prone to too many verifiable examples to the contrary to be maintain validity.

But stereotypes are everywhere and pushed out by (nearly) everyone. Sometimes all you can do to cope is find little ways of entertaining yourself.

I had a boss who used to ask me about what he referred to as "Urban Black" slang (not to be confused with "Rural Black," I guess). And while it wasn't as offensive as if he'd say, asked me to shine his shoes and do a jig, his outlook was still pretty tone deaf. He did appear to be genuinely curious, but it was a curiosity fueled by a racist mindset.

This was a couple years before the American version of the Office, but the character Darryl (played by Craig Robinson) and I had the same approach. If someone ask dumb questions, then by all means, give them dumb answers.

In this case, I told my boss that the use of a certain horrific epithet as a term of familiarity was simply a case of him mishearing. With a perfectly straight face, I let him know that the Black people he'd heard on his way into the office weren't saying what he'd thought they were saying. They weren't referring to each other with that notoriously incendiary epithet. They were referring to each other as "nickels."

Not all bigots wear sheets or burn crosses. The majority of American bigots merely harbor attitudes grounded in ignorance. One of the biggest problems with addressing contemporary problems with bigots is the lack of nuance. All bigotry is negative, but it's not all hate crimes and supremacy advocates. By lumping everything in together, we get a general conflation where if something isn't the extreme, many mistakenly believe that it's not still indicative of that negativity.

I never confronted my EP or old boss about their insensitivity. And I never will. Even if I had then, or if for some bizarre reason, decided to do so now, there'd be no point. It wouldn't undo what had been done, and it's extremely unlikely they'd understand what they did or why they did it.

Aversive racism difficult to absorb by those who engage in it, as by definition, the behavior is predicated on avoidance. And it's even more difficult to combat when you're on the receiving end. The best you can hope for is that the transgressions are as innocuous as an obtuse EP or an out-of-touch old man.

BLACK NERD, BLUE BOX

DOCTOR WHO

"All right let's wrap this up."

"How should I close it out."

"Well, let's talk about Doctor Who."

"I'm with that."

Doctor Who first aired on November 23, 1963. That's exactly sixteen years, one month, and twenty-nine days before I was born. It would take another seven years or so after I was born, before I saw my first episode, Paradise Towers. Since then, Doctor Who has been a constant throughout my life."

The stories have made me laugh, made me upset, made me roll my eyes, given me nightmares, given me thousands of hours of entertainment and support. I'm pretty sure it's the longest-running genre shows, edging out Star Trek by just a couple years.

This fact is even more impressive when you consider that the first run was 26 years, then it went on hiatus for seven years, then had a TV movie, then went on hiatus again for another nine years, and then when the series did return to regularly scheduled, episodic television it became even more popular!

It's a bit daunting to try and explain fully why I love Doctor Who. Even after all these years, The Doctor is still an unquestionably distinctive, and indisputably heroic figure.

The Doctor is the very definition of multidimensional characterization. The Doctor can be, has been, and of course, will likely continue to be witty, sharp, funny, empathetic, angry, dangerous, adventurous, alluring, comical, and infinitely relatable.

For awkward nerds like me, Doctor Who is more than just escapist, sci-fi/fantasy. The Doctor is the outsider's outsider. The epitome of brains over brawn and self-acceptance. When Whovians find themselves in challenging situations in the real world, we often ask ourselves: what would The Doctor do?

My connection to Doctor Who wasn't like my relationship with Star Trek. Star Trek was my social life. The crew of the Enterprise were the friends I didn't have. When my mother was diagnosed with breast cancer the first time, Kirk inspired me to keep going. Spock helped me to stay focused at school. Bones, Scotty, and Sulu kept me entertained, and Uhura comforted me.

But the Doctors, and various companions, and if I'm going to be completely honest, even some of the villains and adversaries- they were aspirational. The best way I can explain it is that Star Trek helped me save for a new bicycle. Doctor Who was the reason I wanted to ride it.

Perhaps the way Doctor Who helped me the most is that it taught me that failure is key to success. Nobody gets it right the first time every time. A lot of people don't get it right the second time either…hell, there are people that don't get it right after the fiftieth or even fifty-thousandth time.

But you can't stop just because it didn't work. You can't stop just because the kids laugh at you. You can't stop because people exclude you based on your skin color, or height, or weight, or musical tastes, or clothing choices. You keep going until you get it right.

We're not Gallifreyan. Unlike the Doctor, we only have this one incarnation, and a very finite amount of time with it, so if nothing else, remember that

There are things we have to do, and things we get to do, so let's do them all…

BLACK NERD, BLUE BOX

ABOUT THE AUTHOR

T. Aaron Cisco is a contemporary Afrofuturist, musician, and award-winning television producer. He is also a contributing writer for TwinCitiesGeek.com, with a focus on TV, Race & Culture. His other works include Teleportality, Dragon Variation, The Preternaturalist, Shadow of the Valley, and Big Ass Aliens.

Made in the USA
Lexington, KY
14 December 2019